A.R.R.E.S.T

Acknowledge – Repent – Renounce – Educate – Seek – Totally Free

A FORMULA FOR TOTAL DELIVERANCE

By CoPastor/Evangelist Cynthia L. Butler

xulon PRESS

Copyright © 2010
by CoPastor/Evangelist Cynthia L. Butler

A.R.R.E.S.T
by CoPastor/Evangelist Cynthia L. Butler

Printed in the United States of America

ISBN 9781609570774

All rights reserved solely by the author. The author guarantees all contents are original and do not infringe upon the legal rights of any other person or work. No part of this book may be reproduced in any form without the permission of the author. The views expressed in this book are not necessarily those of the publisher.

Unless otherwise indicated, Bible quotations are taken from the King James Version.

www.xulonpress.com

DEDICATION

This book is dedicated to my wonderful, supportive husband, Pastor Eric Butler, a true man of God. Only God could have brought us together and made us a team. Thank you for letting me be myself!

Thank you. I love you very much!

A.R.R.E.S.T

Thank you to my amazing children Erica, Yvette and Sir Jonathan. It has been a blessing to be your mom and watch you grow up. You have been an inspiration and special blessing to my life. Love you, Mom.

Introduction: "Making God Happy"

During the course of our life in Christ we must realize that there are many shifts and changes that place us into a divine level of obedience and anointing that pleases God. When we arrive in that place we are consistently doing those things that please God. That is the exact place where we are "Making God Happy."

If there was ever a great praise unto the Lord that all of us can render unto his throne it would be living a life that makes God happy. Imagine living a life where everything we do pleases God. You wake up in the morning and give God his time in prayer and for a change you're not praying on the way out of the door. That would make God happy. He would say oh my, that was good time together. I love being with you like that! God would be happy.

Making God happy includes being properly prepared for the day's mission. The bible says in all thy ways

A.R.R.E.S.T

Prov 3:6

acknowledge him and he shall direct your paths. Living free from hindrances would allow you to be free in Christ so that whatever God needs you to do in any day, you would be ready. How many times do we hear the instructions of God in our heart and we delay going forth to accomplish that task because we need time to repent of sin or go back home and change clothes. Those small details cause delays in our obedience and should God have an emergency situation to attend to a soul or a righteous principle, we would not be ready. Making God happy requires a ready, on the spot, at any time, let's go-vessel that can hear clearly and obey quickly. That's why we need to ARREST. ARREST is a process of spiritual maintenance that keeps our spirits ready to go whenever and whatever God needs from us, right when God wants us to do it. ARREST makes us ready no matter what our heavenly assignment for the day.

The ARREST formula is the formula for your deliverance and your spiritual preparation that is required for those who want to "Make God Happy!" The formula is simply the basic principles of God for our spiritual maintenance placed in a sequence that allows for a complete process. Many of our efforts to be free from our sins, past failures and hindrances are blocked like a concrete wall by

A.R.R.E.S.T

things in our lives that don't make God happy. In the same light, our preparation for anointed service for God requires that we check that we are ready for high accountability to God for completing all assignments with excellence. God is timely and strategic and our delayed obedience to ministry assignments may cost a soul. The delays of obedience come when we are unsure of the voice of God and need to fleece every instruction from the Father. Whereas fleecing is not always a lack of faith, it does take time. Also, whereas God is always on time and always perfect in execution of his will, we, his vessels and instruments can become hindrances to the purpose of the plan.

Often Sunday morning service at my church finds me working the ARREST process with the pastor and ministers during "altar service." For those who don't know, altar service is when we take time to pray with souls until there is evidence of a breakthrough in their lives. The old church called it "tarrying" or waiting on the Lord. There seems to be a stigma left with that concept that reflects people yelling at you confusing instructions often several at the same time. One would say "let go." Another would say "hold on." Someone else would say, "tell him thank you!" A person behind you would say, "say yes Lord." These would be the altar workers, "working with you." "Working

A.R.R.E.S.T

with you" can be anything from just standing nearby and praying for you, to laying hands on you and rebuking the devil and yelling instructions at you to surrender to the Spirit. The objective of tarrying service seemed to be to wear you out until you totally released to God, if for no other reason, but your natural man was too tired to resist God any longer. It worked too! The altar workers were usually flowing with the spirit of God and would discern that you have reached that point of release. Then they would pray with you for the hand of God to move freely in your heart and fill you with the Holy Ghost. It was powerful and tiring, but it was and still is an effective strategy even today. Sometimes we have been in bondage so long that we have to work hard to get it out.

Tarrying was Jesus' instruction to the disciples during the "upperroom" experience. Although many reject the strategy, praying constantly until evidence of receiving from God takes place, is not a new thing. (Luke 24:49)

Luke 24:49 And, behold, I send the promise of my Father upon you: but tarry ye in the city of Jerusalem, until ye be endued with power from on high. KJV

A.R.R.E.S.T

Tarrying is less effective for many believers today because we are so educated and have such microwave mentalities that the time and effort put into tarrying seems almost barbaric. It's sad though, because I am a witness that it works and however confusing it seems it is ARREST in raw form. It is the power and move of deliverance to those who dare to seek God until he rains righteousness. (Hosea 10:12)

Hosea 10:12 Sow to yourselves in righteousness, reap in mercy; break up your fallow ground: for it is time to seek the Lord, till he come and rain righteousness upon you. KJV

ARREST is definitely a process to rid ourselves of sin and weights that take us out of favor with God. Yet, it is just as much the process to continuously do maintenance on ourselves to be sure we are ready for the next assignment and next spiritual level in God. Every believer needs to ARREST. ARREST is powerful basic training for Christ-like living.

If all believers get comfortable saying that "I need deliverance," then the spiritual maintenance that comes

A.R.R.E.S.T

through ARREST will become everyday equipment for powerful living that "Makes God Happy."

Amen

"ARREST"
(A formula for Deliverance)

A – Acknowledge and Pray

*every weight and sin *look up*

*no more secrets

*stop covering for the devil

R – Repent and Pray

*Godly sorrow

*Take action and change

R – Renounce and Pray

*Disown, detach

*Deface and make your sins and bondage ugly as they truly are

E – Educate and Pray

*Study what the Word of God says against it

*Learn about the challenges

*Spiritual defilement vs. Clean vessel promises

A.R.R.E.S.T

S – Seek God and Pray

*Look for God to show up

T – Totally free! Free indeed! And Praise!

*Everything about that defilement-Be offended

*Hate the sin, hate the smell,

*Hate the objects that represent or remind you,

*Hate what sin does to your life:

mind (intellect), soul (spirit), and body (physical)

ARREST Basic Training
FORMULA "D"
(A formula for Deliverance)

A – Acknowledge and Pray

R – Repent and Pray

R – Renounce and Pray

E – Educate and Pray

S – Seek God and Pray

T – Totally free! Indeed! Praise!

The importance of each step is set in the promises of God. God wants us to understand the extent to which Satan has strategically placed us in bondage. It is imperative that we understand that the chains that we wear on our spirit are for our death, not just our hindrance.

John 10:10 The thief cometh not, but for to steal, and to kill, and to destroy: I am come that they might have life, and that they might have it more abundantly. KJV

The abundant life of Christ is inherent to our being in Christ. It is the purpose and will of God that we be free. Freedom ushers us into intimate and powerful relationship with God. Remember the reason for Christ's death, burial and resurrection is for us to be restored to right relationship with God. Abundant life is not an afterthought; it has always been God's intention from the beginning.

The actions of our will determine how and if deliverance will come. Faith without works is dead. (James 2:26) ARREST is a call to active deliverance!

A-R-R-E-S-T - Step 1

A – Acknowledge and Pray
   *lay aside every weight and the sin
   *no more secrets
   *stop covering for the devil

THE ARREST BREAK DOWN:

~LINE UPON LINE

~PRECEPT UPON PRECEPT

A-R-R-E-S-T with Psalms 51

A – Acknowledge and Pray

<u>Acknowledge</u> – to own, or admit to be true, by a declaration of assent
*lay aside every weight and the sin
*no more secrets
*stop covering for the devil

Ps 51:3-4 For I acknowledge my transgressions: and my sin is ever before me. 4 Against thee, thee only, have I sinned, and done this evil in thy sight: that thou mightest be justified when thou speakest, and be clear when thou judgest. KJV

A.R.R.E.S.T

The process begins with all of us coming to terms with bad decisions, failures and unsanctified behaviors that have cost us greatly. Sins, weights and hindrances will always cause us backsliding behaviors if we don't continuously acknowledge and present them to the Lord for deliverance. We can't keep hiding our shortcomings or faults because of pride or embarrassment. Uncover the tactics of the enemy against your life. If we pretend it's not really there or that it's making no real impact on us, we are only fooling ourselves. We fool ourselves, but we never fool God and Satan certainly recognizes his own handy work. Call it what it is and let's rid ourselves of so many ways we can be defeated in our Christian walk. Acknowledging is a really big step. A necessary and ground breaking step.

The first thing we want to do is to say to ourselves and to God that we have a problem that only God can resolve. We have something holding us back from being the powerful instrument of God that we are called to be and we have had enough! Let's tell God that we are not

A.R.R.E.S.T

covering for Satan any longer and that there is no way that we will continue in our current condition. Amen

The key to this type of confession is total honesty and total surrender. We can never come before God in total surrender if there is a part of our problem that we "kind of like" and really don't want that part to go away. It must be all or all! No other options really work in total surrender. It can't even be all or nothing, because we must have change! We must have deliverance! We must be free! If we don't change we will miss heaven! Give God all of it and let him know we know he knows that it's there. We should feel silly to have thought that God didn't know what is really going on and what is truly in our heart. After all, He is God!

This step of acknowledging our spiritual conditions must be accompanied with prayer. Pray about it! We must make the disgust we have about our condition obvious to God. Show him how disgusted we are that we are in this state after all he has done for us. After all, he sent his only begotten Son so that we wouldn't have to be like we are and here we are anyway. The prayer of acknowledgement says that we have had it, and it's time for change or die seeking change. If we are true to acknowledging, it will be all in our prayer life and all in our conversation.

A.R.R.E.S.T

Sometimes things have been in us and part of us so long we have to say it and pray it over and over again until we grab hold to hope and then faith and then deliverance. We won't give up before we are free. Don't let go, even when we feel better! Hold on until we ARE better…free indeed and totally free!

Receive the Message on
Acknowledge
*no more secrets

Ps 51:3-4 For I acknowledge my transgressions: and my sin is ever before me. 4 Against thee, thee only, have I sinned, and done this evil in thy sight: that thou mightest be justified when thou speakest, and be clear when thou judgest. KJV

"IF WE ARE STILL KEEPING OUR PROBLEM A SECRET AND WE HAVEN'T EVEN TALKED TO GOD ABOUT IT...
WE HAVE NOT ACKNOWLEDGED!

WHEN WE COVER FOR THE DEVIL IT'S JUST LIKE...
~NOT TELLING ANYONE THAT SOMEONE RAPED YOU.
IT ALLOWS THE ENEMY TO FIND ANOTHER VICTIM, BELIEVING THAT YOU WON'T TELL SO THE NEXT PERSON WON'T TELL EITHER.

A.R.R.E.S.T

~WE CARRY THE GUILT FOR SOMEONE ELSE'S SIN. WHEN WE CARRY THE GUILT FOR SOMETHING SOMEONE DID TO US, WE CONDEMN OURSELF, AND WE NEED DELIVERANCE FOR NOT BEING TRUTHFUL. THE VERY SAD THING IS THAT WE LET THE PERSON GET AWAY WITH IT. WE THEN LET THEM OFF THE HOOK AND THEY'RE THE BAD GUYS. THEY ARE THE ENEMY OF OUR SOUL AND WE ARE TAKING THEIR PUNISHMENT. YES, WE FORGIVE AND RELEASE OFFENDERS OF OUR SOULS AND OUR LIVES. BUT WE DO NOT TURN AND TAKE THEIR PUNISHMENT OR CARRY THEIR GUILT. FORGIVING IS RELEASING THEM AND IT IS ALSO RELEASING OURSELVES! IF WE NEVER TELL OR ACKNOWLEDGE WHAT HAPPENED TO US, IT STAYS INSIDE OF US AND BECOMES A ROADBLOCK TO OUR GOD-ORDAINED POTENTIAL.

There is an old song that in time past was heard often in churches, that supports the power of acknowledging. It says; "Now let us have a little talk with Jesus, tell him all about our troubles, he will hear our faintest cry and answer by and by….just a little talk with Jesus, makes it right!" In great simplicity this song tells us to acknowledge

A.R.R.E.S.T

that there is an issue that we need to tell God about. The great thing. He's going to make it right.

You see, I believe in the turning around ministry. I believe that no matter what it is that has been strangling the life out of our walk with God, He can turn it around. No matter how debilitating or how handicapping the issue or problem has been, God can and WILL turn it around. **He will take the bad things of our lives and turn them until they become great testimony and great victory and great ministry in us and through us.** The bible lets us know that what the enemy meant for bad God can make it for our good.

Rom 8:28-29 And we know that all things work together for good to them that love God, to them who are the called according to his purpose. 29 For whom he did foreknow, he also did predestinate to be conformed to the image of his Son, that he might be the firstborn among many brethren. KJV

A.R.R.E.S.T

He promised that all things would work together for our good. Joseph had that testimony concerning the evil deeds of his brothers. All the horrible events of his life produced a great servant of the Lord who saved the lives of several nations. He was rejected, abused, sold to slavery, seduced, forgotten, lied on, imprisoned and more. He went through all that, so that he could become the orchestrator of deliverance during the worse famine in the history of the world in that time. But God moved greatly for him and did "turn it around ministry" in Joseph's life. When time came that he would have opportunity for "payback" for all his brothers did to him, **he had by that time been pre-conditioned through suffering to love his brothers and minister in true forgiveness towards them.** Powerful!

Gen 50:20 But as for you, ye thought evil against me; but God meant it unto good, to bring to pass, as it is this day, to save much people alive. KJV

A.R.R.E.S.T

So let's engage the power of telling God all about our troubles. Tell God about what's troubling our mind, heart, our life. Uncover our sins and weights and let them be visible before God. He will not condemn us. He came to rescue us! Let Jesus make it all right! Acknowledge!

Let's pray "Acknowledge:"

Lord, in the name of Jesus we come together in your name. We touch and agree for the power of your deliverance. We need it right now. We look to you and only you for the deliverance of our soul. Father we just learned about your requirement of acknowledging our sins before you. We understand Father that the offense of our sins hurt you. We are now so aware of the pain that we are causing you by not heeding your word. We want to be obedient servants but our sin is ever before us and we can't come to you in clear conscience. Lord your sacrifice on the cross was for this. We take advantage right now of the blood that you shed for our sins. Wash us Lord. Wash and redeem us from our sin habits. We ask you to forgive us of sin as we totally surrender to your will for our lives. We know that you know what is best for us, so we proclaim our trust in you. You can do anything! We

A.R.R.E.S.T

come boldly before the throne of grace and pray for you to "search me oh God and know my ways." Let deliverance become a part of our lives as we continuously present ourselves before you. Purge us with hyssop and we shall be clean, wash us and we shall be whiter than snow. Only you God can do this and so we place our lives in your hands. Uncover our secrets and deliver us in the mighty name of Jesus. Wash us, cleanse us, move every un-confessed sin and even the weights oh God, so that we can move forward in you. You have promised us power from on high. We seek that power. You promised life more abundantly. We seek that life. You promised to be our redeemer. We ask you to change us. We take to heart this first step of this process and believe that we will be changed from this day forth. In Jesus' name we pray. Now I thank you for it God. I thank you because you are faithful, so I believe my request has been heard and I receive the change I need to please you. Thank you Lord. Thank you Father. Glory to your matchless name! Glory and honor belongs to you who after knowing our condition, you still love us! You still Bless us! You still intercede for us! You Lord give us the victory in all these things. Thank you. Amen.

A-R-R-E-S-T - Step 2

R – Repent and Pray
<u>Repent</u> – to feel pain, sorrow, or regret for something one has done or left undone, to change.
*Godly sorrow
*Take action and change

THE ARREST BREAK DOWN:

~LINE UPON LINE

~PRECEPT UPON PRECEPT

R – Repent and Pray

<u>Repent</u> – to feel pain, sorrow, or regret for something one has done or left undone, to change.

*Godly sorrow

*Take action and change

2 Chronicles 7:14 If my people, which are called by my name, shall humble themselves, and pray, and seek my face, and turn from their wicked ways; then will I hear from heaven, and will forgive their sin, and will heal their land. KJV

A.R.R.E.S.T

Receive the Message on Godly sorrow (Repent)

"THE KEY TO GODLY SORROW IS NOT THAT YOU FEEL SORRY FOR YOURSELF… IT'S THAT YOU FEEL SORRY FOR HOW YOU HURT GOD AND DISRESPECTED GOD AND DISHONORED GOD'S LOVE FOR YOU AND DISREGARDED WHAT CHRIST DID ON THE CROSS FOR YOU! THAT SHOULD MAKE YOU FEEL SORRY ENOUGH TO CHANGE! GODLY SORROW

REPENT

The power of repenting is that it jumpstarts the reconnection needed when a covenant or heart agreement has been broken. This is especially amazing when the parties are completely reconciled in their relationship as if no breach ever occurred. It's awesome to see and life changing. to feel...the power of reconciliation through repentance.

The 2 Chronicles 7:14 scripture is so revealing of what true repentance brings with its process. The motion begins with conviction. Conviction is that spiritual alarm system that God puts in the hearts of his children. It's that pulling of heart strings that lets us know that something is wrong and God is not pleased. **Conviction is God's tool to let us feel uncomfortable with things that aren't in his will for us.** It is opposite of Satan's tool of condemnation. Condemnation comes to pull us down and bring a spirit of defeat upon our hearts that makes us feel defeated and hopeless.

A.R.R.E.S.T

God's convictions are based on our knowing the truth of God and the instructions of God. It may feel uncomfortable but it is to push us forward and not downward. The power of repentance is brought to us by the blood of Jesus Christ. Through the sacrifice of Christ on the cross we can now come boldly before the throne of grace. No person has to ever qualify us before God again for we are qualified through the blood sacrifice of Christ. That's why we are so bold now.

Acts 3:19 19 Repent ye therefore, and be converted, that your sins may be blotted out, when the times of refreshing shall come from the presence of the Lord; KJV

Paul had spent many verses prior to this one telling of Christ's death and celebrating his resurrection. He was speaking to those who didn't believe Christ was the son of God, who without conscience wrongly crucified him. He told them that they were guilty but also ignorant of the purpose of God through Christ. Then he provides God's remedy...repent. He gave them the answer to actions done in ignorance, actions done against God and actions that just might have been done on purpose...REPENT.

A.R.R.E.S.T

Paul taught us all a powerful lesson that shows that being sorry without being changed is not repentance. He instructed the guilty to repent and "be converted" or be changed. **He showed them through this that repenting is not enough. There must be change.** We must be sorry for sin and offense to God, but it is not enough! There is a "be converted" clause in God's requirements for being freed from the penalty of sin. Change! Change of mindset, heart, intention and everything else that goes along with it. ARREST it until it is completely turned around and no longer a part of our being. That is what God is looking for.

Our great and forgiving God is not giving us any excuse. Repentance requires change. No matter how hard it is for us, it's required. The truth is those things that seem harsh requirements from God are usually made hard because we are resisting the truth that empowers us to change. If with each conviction you have an excuse or an explanation, you are resisting the power of the truth of God. We don't need to explain to God, he was there. The bible lets us know that he is "Beholding the evil and

33

A.R.R.E.S.T

the good." He knows who said what and who did what and what you did when it was done. No need to think that explaining it to God is going to change his requirements. REPENT, AND BE CONVERTED, THAT YOUR SINS MAY BE BLOTTED OUT.

The end of the process is an overlooked item that makes the repenting and converting part so worth it. God is promising us that he would walk through the process with us so that in that very moment we are converted he uses his blood eraser and clears our slate. He wipes our record clean through the blood. Christ gives us eternal life through his blood. The way we can ever be perfect or acceptable or worthy or anything good in the presence of the almighty God, is that we have the blood-covering speaking for our lives. God honors and values the sacrifice of his Son, Jesus Christ. **The cross was a very, very big deal to God!** Through that horrible act we gained access to the favor and acceptance of God. The veil was ripped and now we can go to God for ourselves. But that's not all. Acts 3:19 tells of a celebration at the end of the repentance process that many forget. God refreshes us and restores us through an awesome flow of his presence at the time when the blood has once again rescued us. The time of refreshing

34

A.R.R.E.S.T

that comes from the presence of the Lord is there every time a true repentance has been engaged. That is the time of refreshing. God accepts our apology. Then Christ cleans and blots out our sin and offense. Then the Holy Ghost, the power and presence of God moves upon us and refreshes our spirit and restores our relationship into right standing with God. Oh my goodness, what a dramatic and powerful process... REPENTANCE.

There is sadness though. Because many run away from the process and then sin takes root and produces some terrible fruit that makes change so much more difficult. If sin and offense is not dealt with quickly it becomes this highway for the enemy to attack, distract and misuse you! Waiting is really bad! Repentance must be quick. Then it has not had a chance to be tainted and infect other parts of your life, heart and spirit. The longer sin remains unattended in our lives, the more it produces and reproduces until it can fully take over. The intention of Satan is to steal, kill and destroy. He never deviates from his purpose.

John 10:10 The thief cometh not, but for to steal, and to kill, and to destroy : I am come that they might have life, and that they might have it more abundantly. KJV

A.R.R.E.S.T

Sin always comes to kill you. But Christ counteracts that by letting us know that he comes to bring life and that more abundantly. So repent and be converted. Let the refreshing presence of the Lord restore you to God. It is soooooo worth it!

Every time we sin we hurt God's heart. So let's apologize to God, change and be refreshed in his presence. REPENT.

LET'S PRAY "REPENT:"

Father we bless your righteous name and praise you for being our God. What an amazing privilege to have you as Lord over our lives. We know that you are God and we are your children, but Father we have done wrong and we know that it hurts you. Lord we have done things that you told us not to do and now we need you to help us. God there is no way out of this except that you forgive us and start us over.

Lord we are so sorry for sinning. We are so sorry for not obeying you. We are so sorry for being slow to move when you told us to go. Forgive us. Lord we are sorry that we ignored your warnings that the enemy was tricking and trapping us. We followed our lust of the eye, we

A.R.R.E.S.T

had pride of life, and we had lust of the flesh. There's no excuse that will make us right. There's nothing to explain, Lord. We were wrong. You did not fail us, we have failed you. After all that Jesus did for us, we have failed you once again. Please forgive us and make us over.

We pray for the blood of Jesus Christ to take our sin, our offense and cleanse us from all unrighteousness. Make us clean again. Make us clean like you did when we first gave our lives to you. You washed our hearts. You washed our minds. You washed our spirits and made us clean before you. Lord do that again. Lord wash us again. Lord make us your children of favor again. We are so sorry that we ever sinned. We bind the devil that our sin gave entrance to. Our sin opened the door for the enemy to attack us and make things worse. Lord forgive us. We cast out the spirit of habits in the name of Jesus! Lord we cast out the spirit of gossip, lying and dishonesty, in the name of Jesus. Lord we cast out every spirit, deceitful thought and action Satan has spoken in our lives. We renounce his ownership of any space within our minds, hearts and spirits. We declare the blood of Christ and ask in the powerful name of Jesus...Lord, restore us to our rightful place in you. We repent, we choose to change and we thank you now for refreshing and restoring us.

A.R.R.E.S.T

Thank you Father, for the power of your presence to forgive us! Thank you Lord, for the power of your presence to change us! Glory! Honor! Unto you Lord who is right now restoring us. Thank you Lord. Thank you Jesus! I'll praise you and remember this moment! I'll praise you and know that you have once again been faithful to our covenant. Thank you Lord, for taking us back and refreshing us and restoring us! We believe and declare in your name that it is done, right now. We thank you. Amen!

Prayer
11/29/12

A-R-R-E-S-T - STEP 3

R – Renounce and Pray

Renounce – to give up a habit or practice, to deny all responsibility for or allegiance to, to give up formally (a right, claim, or trust)
Syn: abandon, abjure, disown, disclaim, abdicate, forsake (Webster's New Universal Unabridged Dictionary, 1983)
*Disown, detach
*Deface and make your sins and bondage ugly as they truly are.

THE ARREST BREAK DOWN:
~LINE UPON LINE
~PRECEPT UPON PRECEPT

R – Renounce and Pray

Renounce – to give up a habit or practice, to deny all responsibility for or allegiance to, to give up formally (a right, claim, or trust)

Syn: abandon, abjure, disown, disclaim, abdicate, forsake (Webster's New Universal Unabridged Dictionary, 1983)

*Disown, detach

*Deface and make your sins and bondage ugly as they truly are

Ezra 10:11-14 Now therefore make confession unto the LORD God of your fathers, and do his pleasure: and separate yourselves from the people of the land, and from the strange wives. 12 Then all the congregation answered and said with a loud voice, As thou hast said, so must we do. 13 But the people are many, *and it is a time of much rain, and we are not able to stand without, neither is this a work of one day or two: for we are many that have transgressed in this thing. 14 Let now our rulers of all the congregation stand, and let all them which have taken strange wives in our cities come at appointed times, and with them the elders of every city, and the judges thereof, until the fierce wrath of our God for this matter be turned from us. KJV*

RECEIVE THE MESSAGE ON RENOUNCING

Every act against the will and ways of God allow a doorway for Satan to enter and attack our mind and spirit.

Renouncing is taking all rights of passage from Satan. He can't go and come as he pleases any more. The door is shut and locked by the blood of Christ that washes away the penalty of our sins.

Rom 6:16-20 16 Know ye not, that to whom ye yield yourselves servants to obey, his servants ye are to whom ye obey; whether of sin unto death, or of obedience unto righteousness? 17 But God be thanked,

A.R.R.E.S.T

that ye were the servants of sin, but ye have obeyed from the heart that form of doctrine which was delivered you. 18 Being then made free from sin, ye became the servants of righteousness. 19 I speak after the manner of men because of the infirmity of your flesh: for as ye have yielded your members servants to uncleanness and to iniquity unto iniquity; even so now yield your members servants to righteousness unto holiness. 20 For when ye were the servants of sin, ye were free from righteousness. KJV

We are no longer servants of sin, but servants of God!

Satan is no longer our lord (boss) but we voluntarily take Jesus as Lord and Savior over our lives.

The key of renouncing is to know that to whom we yield ourselves, that person, habit, tendency becomes our boss. If we submit to Jesus he becomes our boss. That's what being LORD means; he is in control. True ownership must belong to God and nothing or no one else. **The power of ARREST is**

A.R.R.E.S.T

that we end up totally as God's possession. That he and he only is our Lord. Renouncing says that every time we find that we have something other than God manipulating our mind, spirit, body, life and/or decisions we must renounce that ownership by walking that issue through the process of ARREST. Not only do we have to know that only God is in control of us, but that we make anything and everything that is not in alignment with God and his purpose for us uncomfortable and unwelcomed. Renounce it and disown the things that we once allowed to separate us from God. It's time to make that interruption or distraction so unwanted, so ugly, so disgusting that we do everything it takes to get free from it. The influence of habits, unclean thoughts, wrong intentions and the like can make pleasing God difficult. Equally as important, sins, habits, weights all decrease our power in and with God. If we really want to live the abundant life and make heaven our final destination, we must make everything in our earthly life less important than what we need for our heavenly reward. Renounce, disown, disqualify, detest anything that would cause you to miss heaven and miss blessings

A.R.R.E.S.T

down here. **Jesus has promised us so many amazing and powerful things in this life!** Once we turn from sinful living and be transformed by the power of God, we need to make that transformation our state of being. We become stable in that area of deliverance and growth so that we can move forward in God. Renouncing is like closing the door to the enemy. The door has a sign prominently placed in bold letters saying; "ENEMY DO NOT ENTER!"

Romans 12:1-2

When we really want to take away the allure of something that is not good for us it works well to make that thing unattractive in our mind and heart. When something is nasty we will never crave for its flavor. If the mind understands the deadly end of a dangerous act, the heart begins to beat fast when that thing comes to close. When a Christian begins to notice the patterns and habits that are creating weakness in his/her relationship with Christ, the cause of the pattern/habit becomes the enemy. It must be ugly.

I have listened to people reminisce about their past lives as if it was the best time of their lives. That scares me. It's frightening because discussing the past seems to be enticing them to remember and talk about in a way

A.R.R.E.S.T — Romans 6:23

that shows all that it's not ugly to them. It's not weighing its true weight in the eyes of the person telling the story. Sometimes it sounds like a regretful fantasy that was snatched from their grips in the prime of life. Whereas the truth of the matter is that sin equals death. The reality is that had that fantasy continued, it would have killed them; naturally and spiritually. The question then is why aren't they regretful? Why isn't that time of sinful living ugly and distasteful? Why isn't it ugly?

Sin is ugly — Romans 6:23

Until sin and the offense it brings to God's heart become ugly to us Satan has an inroad to our strength. *Give no place to the devil.* Inroads or doors are how the enemy enters and exits our lives. We need to not only shut the door, but we need to eliminate the door and tear down the road. Everywhere there is a pathway to our spirit that's the place where ARREST must be engaged! We should be protected and completely under the cover of the blood of Christ which serves as our justification before God. Renouncing any inroad or doorway to our spirit is what the word of God means when God tells us to resist the devil.

Zech 3:1-2 And he shewed me Joshua the high priest standing before the angel of the Lord, and Satan standing at his right hand to resist him. 2 And the

A.R.R.E.S.T

Lord said unto Satan, The Lord rebuke thee, O Satan; even the Lord that hath chosen Jerusalem rebuke thee: is not this a brand plucked out of the fire? KJV

James 4:7 Submit yourselves therefore to God. Resist the devil, and he will flee from you. KJV

Part of the resisting process is the renouncing of Satan's ownership to our souls. **But the truth is that when we give our lives to Christ he becomes Lord over our lives and Satan has no right to control any part of us again.** What I believe happens is that we allow some things in our sinful past to entice us, especially when we are enduring storms or hard times in our lives. The unspoken truth is that the storms in our Christian lives come to make us strong and prepare us for greater purpose in Christ. Yet the deceit of the enemy tells our minds that either we should return to our old ways or we can't get over the

46

A.R.R.E.S.T

hurt, scares and impact of our past. **But let the record show, "Satan is a liar!"**

Let's pray the renounce!

Father we accept you as Lord in our lives. We praise you for being the savior of our soul. We acknowledge that we have so much to thank you for, especially for your life that you gave for us. Father praise and honor goes to you for who you are. Thank you Lord. We come together in prayer today to touch and agree for total deliverance. We have just learned about renouncing the enemy's hold on our lives. We want you and you only to be Lord over us. We have so many doors from our past decisions that keep allowing the enemy entrance into our minds, our lives and our hearts. Lord we renounce Satan's ownership to any part of us. We surrender to you and give you all authority over our lives. Be Lord over us and let us be free from the things that make us weak and unpleasing to you.

Lord our sins were killing us and you came and gave us life. Please keep our hearts so that we hate evil as you do. Lord give us conviction concerning those things that

A.R.R.E.S.T

are causing the enemy a path to hurt or hinder us. Satan we rebuke you and cast you out of our lives in Jesus' name. We renounce, reject and resist everything that is not what God wants for us. Every item, every problem, every habit, every association, everything and anything not like God we renounce in Jesus' name. Lord we accept your power to be separated and sanctified unto you. We pray this in faith and believe you Lord for the change that is needed to make us free indeed. In the powerful name of Jesus and according to your will for us we pray. Amen!

A-R-R-E-S-T - Step 4
Educate and Pray

Educate – to give knowledge or training to; train or develop the knowledge, skill, mind, or character of, especially by formal schooling or study; teach; instruct.

*Study what the Word of God says about or against it

*Learn about the challenge

*Spiritual defilement verses Clean vessel promises

THE ARREST BREAK DOWN:

~LINE UPON LINE

~PRECEPT UPON PRECEPT

E – Educate and Pray

Educate – to give knowledge or training to; train or develop the knowledge, skill, mind, or character of, especially by formal schooling or study; teach; instruct
*Study what the Word of God says about or against it
*Learn about the challenge
*Spiritual defilement verses Clean vessel promises

There are two things that make God respond; the name of Jesus and His Word. The Word of God is as powerful as a two edged sword.

Heb 4:12 For the word of God is quick, and powerful, and sharper than any two-edged sword, piercing even to the dividing asunder of soul and spirit, and of the joints and marrow, and is a discerner of the thoughts and intents of the heart. KJV

A.R.R.E.S.T

The Bible which is the word of God makes understanding what God wants of us so clear. It empowers us to access God's power through our faith.

Rom 10:17 So then faith cometh by hearing, and hearing by the word of God. KJV

HEBREWS 11:6

The power of the word of God is the foundation of our faith in God. We should never make the mistake of having faith in things, concepts, objects or even people. True faith is belief in God and his word. Faith says that God will do what he said he would. Faith in God is more than believing in a greater power. Although the Almighty God is the greater power, some have taken the concept of greater power and not identified that power as God. Therefore we must clearly identify that our faith is in the true and Living God, the father and creator of us all. Amen We must direct our faith to be in God, what he said, what he can do and ultimately, faith in who God is.

If we have faith in healing that is not true faith. True faith is placed in God who is our healer. If we have faith that we will keep our job, that is not having true faith. True faith is in God who is our provider. Through God's provision we have favor with our employer. Having faith in

Thank You Jesus

A.R.R.E.S.T

someone we love is not faith. True faith is in God who is love! Misdirected faith can be faith wasted on things and people who can't do what you believe they can. True faith is in God. **True faith is in the power and omnipotence of God. It's his ability that makes believing the unbelievable so reasonable.** He can do it. Is there anything too hard for God? Num 23:19

It is the will of God that we have his word within us to keep us knowledgeable of what his will is. Having the word of God living inside of us will take away the wondering and searching that many do to "find themselves." The search is short and sweet when the word of God is leading and guiding our footsteps. It is our goal to have the word on the "inward parts" so that the outward parts will obey.

Ps 51:6 Behold, thou desirest truth in the inward parts: and in the hidden part thou shalt make me to know wisdom. KJV

A.R.R.E.S.T

God is a Lord of truth. His word is truth. When we learn the word of God and put it into our hearts, we have done what is best for us all. Knowing the word is the beginning of wisdom. Someone once told me that wisdom is having knowledge and knowing what to do with it. Wisdom helps us make godly decisions and choices. No wonder those who don't serve God have so much confusion. The word of God is a confusion blaster. He has given us a sound mind; through his word. II Tim 1:7

John 5:38-39 And ye have not his word abiding in you: for whom he hath sent, him ye believe not. 39 Search the scriptures; for in them ye think ye have eternal life: and they are they which testify of me. KJV

II Tim 3:16

In the bible, John the fifth chapter is helping us to understand that we must receive the word of God with a mindset of Christ. The scriptures instruct us to "Let this mind be in you which was also in Christ Jesus."

Having the mind of Christ is having the word in our hearts until it dictates our behaviors.

A.R.R.E.S.T

Then we become one of those who "testifies" of Christ as we live day to day. Learning and living the word provokes Christ to call out to the world saying, they are mind. See the way they live. They know my word; it's in their hearts. They know who I am!

Therefore the ARREST step of Educate, really says this... Get a word on our issues! Find out what God says about it! Find out which side of the issue is God's side. We should not come before the throne of God empty handed when we pray. We need to come before him with his word of promise in our hearts. "Get a word on it" and hold God to his promise. Grab hold to depression and declare the promise of peace that passes all understanding that God gives to us. Take marriage problems and speak against it, tell division in our marriages that whom God has put together let no man set asunder. The step of Educate in the ARREST process says that God will honor his word and we need to be free. He will prove his word by setting us free. So naturally we need to get a freeing word and hold it high before God and ask him to do as he promised! So our prayer for educate is to ask God to teach us his truth; his word is truth. Ps 86:11 Ps 119:26

Often in workshops or messages I teach hearers to find a scripture to set you free and write it on a note and

A.R.R.E.S.T

post on the bathroom mirror and read it as you prepare for your day. Take another note, write a promise from God for your life on it. Place it on the dashboard of your car or inside the book you are reading while riding the train and don't let his promises out of sight. I encourage every believer to grab hold of a word and keep in front of your face until it becomes a part of you. The word of God is right, the promises of God are sure. We must get a WORD; a scripture, to lift above our problems and hold God to his promises. He will never fail! God is able and his word is unfailing. God has a consistent record and failing is not his testimony. **GOD WILL DO EVERYTHING HE PROMISED!**

LET'S PRAY "EDUCATE:"

Ps 86:11 Teach me thy way, O Lord; I will walk in thy truth: unite my heart to fear thy name. KJV

Lord God of all that is true we come in praise and honor of your holy name. You are the God of truth and power. We exalt you among the people and among the nations.

A.R.R.E.S.T

You are worthy of all praise and we glorify you right now. Your word is what we seek today Lord. We need a word from you. Father let there be a yearning placed within our hearts to know your word. When the enemy comes against us we want to know what your word says that gives us power over the enemy's tactics. In the name of Jesus, give us an understanding of your word so that we will know you Lord all the more.

Father every area in our lives requires us to continue to grow and maintain a standard of holiness. We can't do that without your word. Teach us the word against defeat. Teach us your word against weakness. Lord, teach us the word of power and strength! In your name we can be all that you are calling us to be …by the power of your word. Lord, teach us thy way. Let your word be a lamp unto our feet and a light unto our pathway. We want to know where to go and we desire Lord to have clear directions from you. Your word is our direction. We want you to be a living word within us, each and every day. We pray in your mighty name. Amen!

ARREST – STEP 5

S – Seek God and Pray

<u>Seek</u> – to search; to explore or investigation

*Look for God to show up

THE ARREST BREAK DOWN:

~LINE UPON LINE

~PRECEPT UPON PRECEPT

S – Seek God and Pray

<u>Seek</u> – to search; to explore or investigation

*Look for God to show up

(handwritten: Read entire chapter)

1 Chronicle 16:11 Seek the LORD and his strength, seek his face continually. KJV

Receive a message on: Seek

1 John 4:10 10 Herein is love, not that we loved God, but that he loved us, and sent his Son to be the propitiation for our sins. KJV

Jesus has already done the preparation for our deliverance. He was the ultimate sacrifice long ago so we can have personal access to God today. We are talking about seeking God. **He said if we seek him, we'll find him.** So we pray and we seek. We pray again and we seek again. We do it again and again until we experience a change. Seek the lord until he rains righteousness on us.

Hosea 10:12 Sow to yourselves in righteousness, reap in mercy; break up your fallow ground: for it is time to seek the LORD, till he come and rain righteousness upon you. KJV

We will need to continue to seek him until He rains his righteousness on us. Righteousness is the power of being right-God's way. Seeking is as if we are holding our needs in the palms of our hands and lifting everything up before God's face. Seeking is giving God full view of ourselves and the things that concern us. We want him to see what is in our hands. We seek him until he takes care of each item and our hands are once again empty. All the while we give him praise because we have no doubt that he can and handle things for us.

We too often invest time, energy and resources into things that take us away from the power of what Jesus did for us on the cross. **Preparation has already been made for us to be free and live abundantly.** We must now align our lives with our predestined state of living. He said, behold I stand at the door and knock and if any man hear my voice, and open the door, I will come into him and sup with him. We have access through Christ to God! When we get into his presence he doesn't want to haggle or debate over what we can do and still be saved. He is not going to spend his time identifying the line that separates us from sinful living. I believe God wants us to stay away from the line. He wants us hot or cold. He wants to sup with us and commune with us daily.

What is sup with him? It means He's going to start working in us and be who he is for us. We seek God by faith, yes, but he said if we seek him, we will find him. We are not playing a game of hide and seek. God is standing in clear view waiting for us to come out of the shadows of our sin and our past. Keep reading the word of God until we find him. So if we left before we found him, we left empty because we didn't seek him long enough. We don't have to wonder if we have found God. If we are asking the question, then we haven't found him yet! If we stopped seeking before he brought it to pass, we're not done. **When we find God, we will know it!** He will become plain and clear into our view; no disguise, no mystery. If it's not clear, then know that it's not God. When Jesus touched the eyes of the blind man with clay he made from his spit, he asked him, "how do you see?" The man said that he seen men as trees. Jesus in essence said go back and wash until you see me clearly. When all was done the blind man's testimony was that he seen men as they are. Then Jesus declared he was healed. It makes me wonder how often Jesus has been standing right in front of me and I couldn't see him clear enough to know that it was him. Nonetheless, keep seeking until you see him clearly, understand him fully and know him intimately. When we freely release that hindering and limiting offense in our lives unto God we will not be mistaken when the power of deliverance comes to our lives. We don't have worry, we don't have fear, all we have to do is just seek God until we feel his refreshing rain fall on our lives! There is no good thing God will withhold from those who seek him.

A.R.R.E.S.T

So in circumstances where we have had a pattern of failure and we realize that we have not fallen today, then we know we've found God. Also, if we did not say the wrong thing today, where we have been saying the wrong thing consistently, we know seeking God has again paid off for us. When God's presence comes, we are delivered.

For in the presence of the Lord is fullness of joy. **So when we are seeking God for our total deliverance we don't stop until we have evidence that God has truly changed us.** God will become evident in our strength, in our mindset and in our actions. We are free and we don't have to worry about it ever again as long as we leave it in God's hands and don't take it back. We filled empty spaces with the power of God where weakness use to reside. stay with our faith; now things don't worry us. Faith says it's changed; it's not happening that way anymore, that's not me any more. So when we prayed for God to stop our lusting eyes from wondering, now we keep our flesh under control we have evidence that God has done us again. We have to seek

A.R.R.E.S.T

God, believing his word by faith. But it's more than raw faith. It's faith plus true hope. The scripture tells us to hope in God. Hope is a necessary part of faith. If seek God and really don't believe we will find him, we will walk right by him and miss our day of change and power. If faith is the evidence of things hoped for, then hope must be first and then faith brings evidence.

Let me tell you a story of a time God taught me that I needed something more than just my faith. I always believe faith was all I needed. But God revealed to me one powerful day, that hope is a necessary thing for all those who seek him with their whole heart.

The HOPE REVELATION

When I was ministering in New York there was part of the service where the church was having the youth leader minister to the youth. It was youth night. Their youth minister was ministering to the youth and she was very good at it and she was moving in the power of God as she spoke to the children. Then all of the sudden she looked up and then yelled, "oh God, my mother is here!" She began to cry frantically and began to praise the Lord for her mother being in the room. She became hysterical

A.R.R.E.S.T

with praise and those who knew her began to praise the Lord with her. I began to look around to find out who her mother was and why this kind of reaction was happening.

I was sitting on the front row and saw her mom who caused this hysterical praise coming down the aisle. I really didn't understand. But then as I saw her mother God began to speak to my heart. In the midst of this unbelievable, frantic praise God spoke to me. God knew I had been praying for my unsaved family. He knew that it was often a hard burden to keep having faith without evidence year after year. God understood that I needed something else to help keep my faith strong and unwavering.

This sister was in the middle of preaching and this amazing praise broke out. **It came out of her belly like a roar and a scream because she had been seeking God for her mother and even before her mother could reach the altar she could see it so real!** She not only had faith, but her hope was being manifested as she watched her mother walk into the church.

It was faith plus hope! Faith was made manifest (alive/reality) by the hope she had for God to save her mother.

Then one of the loving sisters in the church went back and began to escort her mother to the altar. Her mother who had previously told her she was not coming to "that church," was crying and walking to the altar and the power of God was moving out of this amazing praise. We found out later that her mother had never heard or saw her daughter minister and the power of her daughter's anointed ministry hit her right in the heart.

When I saw her mother coming down the aisle, my spirit got pricked. Here is what God showed me. God said to me is that this is what I needed. I've always had faith that God will save my family, but I did not have hope! At the moment I saw that mom, I was relating to what it would feel like to have my unsaved family come to surrender totally to God. So when I saw her mother coming down the aisle with her eyes filled with repenting tears, God revealed the truth to me. I had faith, but I must also have HOPE. I needed to be able to see in my mind's eye...that the bondage my family has been in all of my life, would be released some powerful day. They would one day walk down the aisle and give themselves to God with all their mind, soul and strength. I needed to believe it until I was full of hope. I needed a visual of hope for my families' spiritual freedom. I needed to see it with my faith.

Hope is the eyes of our faith!

I needed to seek God in faith until I could see it, until I could praise him like it was happening right at that moment of faith. I never before had a twinkling of vision of what it would look like to have my family walk down that isle. Yet, right there as I watched this mother come to the altar with such emotion I understood what God was requiring of me. Even if I wasn't there when it happened, I needed to be able to see it so real that I could feel the joy and power of God. I needed to see God doing work on my family until it transformed my spirit. Faith was no longer enough. The truth is that I was seeking God, but I didn't have true faith.

Our faith needs to give evidence and substance to our hope in God. We need hope so that we could feel it, and see it, and praise God for it just like it was happening right when we believe! The scriptures request hope of us in Psalm 42:5. (See also Ps. 42:11, Ps. 43:5)

Ps 42:5 Why art thou cast down, O my soul? and why art thou disquieted in me? hope thou in God: for I

shall yet praise him for the help of his countenance. KJV

That mother came down the aisle and the sisters began to pray with her. Then she turned and hugged her daughter. They began to praise God together and then I had hope. I could see what it would be like because I had hope. So many of us need to ARREST every hindrance in our lives until we know what it will feel like not to have that hindrance. Seek him until we can visualize what it would feel like not to have that burden any more. Seek him until we praise freely over that thing that has not yet disappeared in the natural, but in the spirit we have evidence by the word of God that it is gone. It is over! We are free in deed.

That's what seeking is about. Seek him until we have hope in God ! Seek him until we have evidence that we are delivered. Let's Rejoice like our deliverance is walking down the aisle and we feel the presence of God around us going higher because of our faith. I have to believe in faith until I have a glimpse of what that would look like. Now we have to be able to at least imagine what it would be like to have what we are asking God to do. Now we are seeking! Seek until we say, oh God I thank you, this is exactly what it's going to look like and feel like when we get free, when we get deliverance. Seeking God until we find him is taking in the word of God until we have faith. Then taking our faith and seeking him until we have hope that we can see and feel. We won't leave, won't stop seeking until we know without a doubt that God has it under his complete control. We have hope because we can see it with our faith that the almighty God has delivered us! Don't settle for less. God is going to deliver!

God is going to lighten our load and prepare us for greater praise, greater ministry. Deliverance is just that... God lightening our load. Deliverance is God giving us abundant life through Christ in every area of our lives! Seek him until God lightens the load!

LET'S PRAY "SEEK:"

Thank you Father. Thank you Lord. We give Glory to your all-powerful name. It is you that we seek Lord. It's you. We want to know you in the power of your resurrection. Lord we can't even imagine the power of a relationship based on the power that raised you from the dead. But God that's exactly what we want. We want to understand

A.R.R.E.S.T

who you are beyond the ability of our own minds. We seek you with our hearts. We seek you with all our soul!

There is so much that we need from you, but we take your word to heart and we look for what you want for us. Thy will be done, oh God! Thy will oh God, for our lives and our purpose in you. What do you want us to do Lord. We know that you have the best plan for our lives. So Father we throw away our flawed ideas of what our futures should be like. Father, your plan is what we seek. We want to know what you want us to do. We want to know where you want us to go. Father we want to step off our path and move onto your plathway. We seek by the truth of your word. Lord we pray this and seek this by the sureness of your promises. In the name of Jesus! Lord we hear you knocking at the doors of our hearts and we choose to open the door and let you in. Come in oh God, Come in! We pray for a heart that seeks you always and knows your voice when you speak to us. We pray that it is so, in the mighty name of Jesus. Amen!

<u>ARREST – Step 6</u>
T – Totally free! Free indeed! And Praise!

<u>Totally Free</u> - without limits, boundaries and hindrances
<u>Indeed</u> - completely
*Everything about that defilement—Be offended
*Hate the sin, hate the smell, hate the objects that represent or remind you,
*Hate what it does to your life
*Mind (intellect), soul (spirit), and body (physical)

THE ARREST BREAK DOWN: ~LINE UPON LINE ~PRECEPT UPON PRECEPT

T – Totally free! Free indeed! And Praise!

<u>Totally Free</u> - without limits, boundaries and hindrances

<u>Indeed</u> - completely

*Everything about that defilement—Be offended

*Hate the sin, hate the smell, hate the objects that represent or remind you,

hate what it does to your life

*Mind (intellect), soul (spirit), and body (physical)

John 8:36 If the Son therefore shall make you free, ye shall be free indeed. KJV

1 Chron 4:10 And Jabez called on the God of Israel, saying, Oh that thou wouldest bless me indeed, and

A.R.R.E.S.T

enlarge my coast, and that thine hand might be with me, and that thou wouldest keep me from evil, that it may not grieve me! And God granted him that which he requested. KJV

The prayer of Jabez has been examined by many and has been used in support of many prosperity initiatives. Yet the end request of being kept from evil is the totally free concept that we want to understand in greater detail. The prayer is asking for God's favor in several areas. The area of being blessed indeed is the part that many really like. Yet the "indeed" means in everything that God has ordained to be blessed there would be complete and total blessing. Therefore some proclaimers may want to examine their requests to see if it's something that would please them or please God?

You'll know that you are totally free when things don't slip up on you or out of you. For when you are free it's not covered up…it's gone. Then you become stable in God and stabilized against the enemy's attacks.

Hear a word about: STABILIZE!

1 Corinthians 15:58 Therefore, my beloved brethren, be ye stedfast , unmoveable, always abounding in the work of the Lord, forasmuch as ye know that your labour is not in vain in the Lord. KJV

Totally free is about having a state of being stable in God. When true deliverance comes it will stabilize you. If you want a sign or a checkpoint to know if you are really, really free, see if you are stable in that thing. If it is in prayer, are you stable in your prayer life? If it is in keeping your spirit clean, are you stale in cleanliness? If it's being sanctified, are you stable in your sanctification? True deliverance is about being stable and not wavering in our allegiance and faith in Christ. When you reach the status of being totally free you will stabilize in your daily walk with God. You will not be tossed to and fro with every wind and doctrine.

Eph 4:14-15 That we henceforth be no more children, tossed to and fro , and carried about with every wind of doctrine, by the sleight of men, and cunning craftiness, whereby they lie in wait to deceive; 15 But

speaking the truth in love, may grow up into him in all things, which is the head, even Christ: KJV

You will not be sometimes up and sometimes down. Nor will any longer be level to the ground, as they say. When Christ sets you free you will be free indeed! He promised to establish and settle us and we will take that word of promise and be totally free.

1 Peter 5:10 But the God of all grace, who hath called us unto his eternal glory by Christ Jesus, after that ye have suffered a while, make you perfect, stablish , strengthen, settle you. KJV

If we still are not sure how to know when we are "free indeed" we must then be deliberate and strategic. When someone really wants to make sure that he/she does not forget to check on something they make a list. Just like a grocery list helps the shopper make sure that each item is purchased and nothing if forgotten, so we can make a list of those things we believe God to do for us.

A list of those things that we already know is not pleasing to God in our lives is on top of the list. We ARREST it by acknowledging that there are some things that we must continue to perfect in our lives. Sometimes you have to make a list and then consciously check it off when we are set free. When God blesses something that you have written and presented to him in prayer you check it off and give God praise for what he has done for you. Sometimes we miss our blessing waiting for a big bang. The reality of life is that change comes about a little at a time. So if we make a list and present each item in prayer to the Father, knowing how faithful he is, we can begin to check things off as he shows himself mighty on our behalf. He is faithful and just the bible says. He will not forsake us and if we know that he has heard us, the bible says then we know that we shall have what we ask of him. We know then that we will be checking things off the list! There is nothing to hard for God! Listen to the word of God on these principles.

1 John 1:9-10 If we confess our sins, he is faithful and just to forgive us our sins, and to cleanse us from all unrighteousness. 10 If we say that we have not sinned, we make him a liar, and his word is not in us. KJV

A.R.R.E.S.T

Stabilize in Christ

After declaring with the saints a prophetic word heard around the country and heard in our convocation the Lord gave me this message. This message speaks to what to do to stay delivered. This is a message of spiritual maintenance.

Spiritual maintenance is the process of making sure that we attend to our deliverance so that we don't lose it. Sometimes we seem to take for granted that once God delivers us we don't have to attend to that any more. But the bible lets us know that Satan as a roaring lion wonders the earth seeking to devour us. We can't take the chance that something that we thought was over and done with has regrouped or grown back again. We must make sure that we maintain our spiritual advances. We must look to see that the ground around our heart and spirit remains to be good ground.

There is a parable in the bible that symbolizes the difference between good ground and poor ground. Here it would be maintained ground and unattended ground. The parable of the sower.

A.R.R.E.S.T

Matt 13:18-30 Hear ye therefore the parable of the sower. 19 When any one heareth the word of the kingdom, and understandeth it not, then cometh the wicked one, and catcheth away that which was sown in his heart. This is he which received seed by the way side. 20 But he that received the seed into stony places, the same is he that heareth the word, and anon with joy receiveth it; 21 Yet hath he not root in himself, but dureth for a while: for when tribulation or persecution ariseth because of the word, by and by he is offended. 22 He also that received seed among the thorns is he that heareth the word; and the care of this world, and the deceitfulness of riches, choke the word, and he becometh unfruitful. 23 But he that received seed into the good ground is he that heareth the word, and understandeth it; which also beareth fruit, and bringeth forth, some an hundredfold, some sixty, some thirty. 24 Another parable put he forth unto them, saying, The kingdom of heaven is likened unto a man which sowed good seed in his field: 25 But while men slept, his enemy came and sowed tares among the wheat, and went his way. 26 But when the blade was sprung up, and brought forth fruit, then appeared the tares also. 27 So the

A.R.R.E.S.T

servants of the householder came and said unto him, Sir, didst not thou sow good seed in thy field? from whence then hath it tares? 28 He said unto them, An enemy hath done this. The servants said unto him, Wilt thou then that we go and gather them up? 29 But he said, Nay; lest while ye gather up the tares, ye root up also the wheat with them. 30 Let both grow together until the harvest: and in the time of harvest I will say to the reapers, Gather ye together first the tares, and bind them in bundles to burn them: but gather the wheat into my barn. KJV

The ground that is spoken of is your heart. Will you stabilize and allow God to bring good fruit from your life. Hear the word of God and be changed. Be transitioned from where you are to where God wants you to be. Remember there will always be another greater place in God for you. He always will keep moving us forward and upward. The transition is also a transformation. Some time when God begins to use his word to change us we grow so much that we also can't recognize ourselves later.

There have been times when I looked back at some things that happened and I honestly can't believe that I did those things. I remember a time when I felt like I would never stabilize. I would go so far in God and then I would mess up. I would stumble and fall at small things in life that really I should have been seasoned in the Lord enough to not be bothered. But I was more than bothered. Those small things became giant spirit killers. I become stable in the Lord. I remember praying and asking God to stabilize me. I had been in a long season of ups and downs in God and I was tired of having to repent all the time. I would go so far and my pastor would sit me down from ministering because I was too mouthy. I would consecrate and grow and then I would stumble again over things from my past that haunted me. I know now that doors were standing wide open in my life and the enemy was just going and coming as he pleased. When I was strong in the Lord, Satan would leave for a while. He oppressed from the outside, but he didn't have a way inside of me. I resisted the devil and he fled from me just like the bible says.

Yet there were those times, over and over, when residue from my past sins and decisions haunted me and pushed me into depressions, lusts and sins against the God that I love so much. It was tormenting because I really in my heart wanted to be saved and I wanted to be stable in God. I asked God, when would I ever stop falling? I wanted to stop going up and down; I wanted to stabilize!

The end process is to create a mental or literal list of what you are seeking for God to do in your life. Understand God's character and stand upon his promise to be your deliverer and track the goodness of the Lord towards you. The list is an acknowledgment from you to the Lord of the things you know that he wants to be cleared or improved in your life. Let God know that you have read his word and you understand that holiness is right. You know that what the Lord requires of you are simple principles of salvation.

Micah 6:8 He hath shewed thee, O man, what is good; and what doth the Lord require of thee, but to do justly, and to love mercy, and to walk humbly with thy God? KJV

The truth is that all God is requiring of his children is that we be loyal to the principles of righteousness. He wants us to "do justly" and do what's right. He wants us to "love mercy" and minister in love and kindness to others and ourselves. God desires that we know that it's a privilege to be saved and we should always understand how great God's love was that provided such a great salvation.

We didn't deserve God's gift of his son, Jesus Christ. We didn't earn redemption. God in his great love towards us gave us everything we need to please him and inherit eternal life.

2 Peter 1:2-4 Grace and peace be multiplied unto you through the knowledge of God, and of Jesus our Lord, 3 According as his divine power hath given unto us all things that pertain unto life and godliness, through the knowledge of him that hath called us to glory and virtue: 4 Whereby are given unto us exceeding great and precious promises: that by these ye might be partakers of the divine nature, having escaped the corruption that is in the world through lust. KJV

Stabilize. Be strong. Be courageous! ARREST everything in your way!

Eph 6:10-11 Finally, my brethren, be strong in the Lord , and in the power of his might. 11 Put on the whole armour of God, that ye may be able to stand against the wiles of the devil. KJV

A.R.R.E.S.T

IT'S TIME TO PUT IT UNDER ARREST!

LET'S PRAY "TOTALLY FREE:"

Lord Jesus, we just want to be free. God it's so clear to us now why we have been going in circles in our Christian walk with you. God make our steps sure and our pathways clear. Clean up the dibre from our past decisions while we were in sin. This is not the way you want us to live. Lord the truth is you want us to be free even more than we want ourselves to be free.

Before we started we couldn't even admit that we have a problem. Now Lord, we say loud and clear that we have a problem that only you mighty God can fix. Lord before we were slow to repent when we fumbled and when we fell. But God now you have shown us the amazing power that comes through a repentant heart. We didn't know that repentance gave us power with you. Lord we were so blind, we were so unequipped, but not any more. Thank you for that! Hallelujah! We give you glory and praise for taking time to show us. Thank you Lord for bringing this simple, but so powerful process into our lives. Thank you for loving us the way you do.

We don't want anything holding us back from our true purpose and you showed us how to renounce Satan's hold on us. You taught us so easily how to take the enemy's permission slips away so that he nor any other hindrance would have a pathway into our lives. Your presence is over us and your blood covers us and makes us OK. There is nothing that we have done to deserve this, but your unfailing grace is moving on our behalf. Praise your mighty name. We absolutely refuse to stay the way we are. We want to be free. We take your word and hold your promises before your face and ask in Jesus' name for you to do what you said you would do for us. Help us Father to be removed from the weights and sins that so easily beset us and let us be free through your power. Thy word is truth and your promises are sure! We stand firmly on our faith as evidence to our hope in you. For you Lord are able to do exceedingly and abundantly above all that we can ask or think and we are counting on you to be our deliverer and set us free indeed. We pray that you do this for us, in the name of Jesus Christ our Savior. Amen!

ARREST

Arrest: A case study

Vessel: A Struggling Believer:

April's Challenge:

Lack of Faith

ARREST

Arrest: A case study
Vessel: A Struggling Believer:
April's Challenge:
Lack of Faith

A – Acknowledge

April's Prayer: Lord I have a constant battle in my mind and in my heart over faith. I want to believe your word. I want to believe that you can deliver me, heal me and use me, but it's hard. I know myself, I know what I've done. I haven't been able to do it yet, why should I believe that it will get better now. What's different now than before . Lord your word says that without faith it's impossible to please you. Well, I know then that I am not pleasing you. Help me! Deliver me from unbelief.

Action: Friend confronts April not to keep pretending and be saved. April speaks the truth of her faith. *" You know*

A.R.R.E.S.T

what you are so right. I have struggled for as long as I can remember with my faith to live without sin. But pray with me as I'm starting to seek God for more faith. I'm studying the bible. There is a scripture that faith cometh by hearing and hearing by the word of God. So I'm starting with my bible. Then next week I plan to go to bible study and hear more word. I expect things to get better and me to get stronger."

R – Repent

April's Prayer: Lord forgive me. I have not been believing. I have not had faith. Forgive me. I want to do those things that change the way I do things until I walk by faith as your word tells me. Forgive me for my unbelief. Unbelief is sin and I choose you Lord and I choose to live saved.

Action: I'm going to take a scripture each day and focus on believing what the word says. I'm going to start with scriptures that help me get more faith; God's promises. It may only be one scripture a day, but I believe God is going to help me with the rest. I am not going to keep going the way I've been, I'm going to let the promises of

God change me. AND…I am not going to worry about if its going to work. I'm just doing it

April's Case Study: continued

R – Renounce

<u>April's prayer</u>: Lord I acknowledge I have a faith problem. I am not hiding or pretending any more. I have asked you to forgive me and I am moving forward. I don't know how I became so bad at faith, but this is the end. I renounce anything that I have allowed in my life that makes it hard for me to believe your word for my life. I rebuke anything that the devil has planted in my heart or my mind to make it so hard to believe you will help me. I'm no longer owning or responding to the title of not having faith, I renounce that title because it condemns me to be destroyed. I need faith and I'm not taking it lightly that I have not been living by faith. I have faith in you. You never fail and you won't fail me. I give my heart to you Lord in faith, for my faith, in Jesus' name I declare and believe. Amen.

<u>Action</u>: Every time doubt or fear comes to her mind, April will renounce the enemies of her faith and repent for that

A.R.R.E.S.T

specific thing that has been allowed to hinder her. " Lord I feel fear about telling people that I believe you are delivering me. Fear is the enemy of my faith. I renounce and reject what the devil is telling me and I've made up my mind to put my faith in you. I am no longer a slave to fear or doubt. I am free by the power of God. And every time the devil brings me fear, I will not follow it. I believe you can change my life so that I can live by faith. In Jesus' name! Right now!.

E – Educate

April's prayer: Lord show me scriptures of promise of faith. I want to learn them and know them and use them against my doubts and fears.

Action: Open the bible and write down every scripture I find about faith and having faith in God. Write the scriptures and study them every day. Share what I learn with others; email, letters, phone calls, poems, songs of faith filling all the spaces in my life.

~Heb 11:6 But without faith it is impossible to please him: for he that cometh to God must believe that he

is, and that he is a rewarder of them that diligently seek him. KJV

"I don't have an option, if I want to please God, I have to have faith in him."

~ Rom 1:17 For therein is the righteousness of God revealed from faith to faith: as it is written, The just shall live by faith. KJV

"I choose to make Faith a way of life. I believe God"

S – Seek

April's Prayer: Lord thank you for your forgiveness, thank you for delivering me from fear and doubt. I want to be your servant of faith. Help me to learn your word to increase my faith. Help me to rebuke and renounce every behavior, tendency and mindset that does not agree with faith in you. In the name of Jesus, I ask in faith, Amen.

Action: Seeking God is founded in prayer time. April now attends as many of the corporate prayers at church that her work schedule will allow. She has a prayer partner who she prays with once a week. April not only attends prayer but has volunteered to be on the intercessory prayer team and spends one lunch hour a week at the church in noonday prayer. To support her word increase April has purchased bible software to put on her computer to help with researching topics to support her faith.

T – Totally Free

<u>April's Prayer</u>: Lord my heart, mind and soul says yes! Yes Lord, Yes Lord. Thank you for setting me free from fear and doubt. Thank you for forgiving me for unbelief. Thank you for teaching me in your word how to be powerful in my faith. I will continue to practice my faith in every area of my life. Thank you Jesus! Lord I pray that I never forget to seek you in faith and to increase my faith. I choose to live and walk by faith as your word commands. I am free from the bondage and sin of unbelief. I will speak it, share it, testify about it. I am delivered, I am forgiven, I will always be thankful for all that you have done to transform my mind and my life. I will continue in the faith and I will never return to unbelief. With your help Lord, I am a woman of faith!

A.R.R.E.S.T

<u>Action</u>: Testimony service – "Saints I just wanted to stand and say that I am free! God has set me free from fear and doubt. He has forgiven me for my unbelief and I am armed with the word and promises of God. Thank God I am free!"

Case study Summary: April finally admitted that she has doubt and fear and just could not believe God. She couldn't live saved and sanctified because she couldn't find any reason God would invest his power in the life of someone like her. She found out that she needed the word of God to have power to change. She found out that not only did she need God to forgive her for unbelief, she needed to forgive herself for self-condemnation. She learned the word that builds faith. She changed her mindset and conversation. She confessed and testified of her lack of faith and declared her new commitment to faith in God. She continues to battle against fear and doubt and consciously walks through the ARREST each time the enemy of faith shows up in her life. April is totally free and she does things that free people do.

Notes: What have you Learned from April's Case?

Arrest: A formula for Deliverance

Insert your case

Arrest: A formula for Deliverance
Insert your case

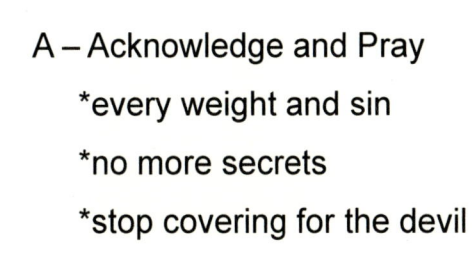

A – Acknowledge and Pray
    *every weight and sin
    *no more secrets
    *stop covering for the devil

    What is it?

How is it effecting your life?

What should be in that space in your life instead?

A.R.R.E.S.T

What do you want to pray and tell God about this?

Insert your case:

R – Repent and Pray

    *Godly sorrow

    *Take action and change

    Tell God what it is?

    Tell God how much you are sorry?

    Pray for God's forgiveness and mercy.

A.R.R.E.S.T

Receive God's forgiveness for your sin.

Confess the changes that will now have to take place in your life.

Insert your case:

R – Renounce and Pray
　*Disown, detach
　*Deface and make your sins and bondage ugly as they truly are

"Sometimes we share our past experiences in sin as glamorous times filled with carefree fun. The truth is that our sin was killing us every day. We had to increase the depth of our commitment to sin to feel satisfaction and soon found ourselves doing things we promised ourselves we would never do. Sin is Ugly! Its only goal is to

A.R.R.E.S.T

destroy your chances to be healed, saved, and set free. I repeat...SIN IS UGLY!

Declare God's promise of freedom over your life. Pray it! & Say It!

Renounce Satan's ownership of your life, mind, heart and spirit. Tell Satan you are no longer his property!

Renounce the guilt of your sin because you are forgiven.

Speak evil of Satan's trap and detach your mind and spirit from evil influences... In Jesus' Name!
(The more detailed you are the more powerful your renouncing becomes) Tell the devil you are not his to boss around any more!

A.R.R.E.S.T

Insert your case:

E – Educate and Pray

*Study what the Word of God says against it

*Learn about the challenges

*Spiritual defilement vs. Clean vessel promises

Research and List Scriptures that empower you against this sin, weight or bondage:

1.

2.

3.

4.

5.

6.

A.R.R.E.S.T

Insert your case:

S – Seek God and Pray

*Look for God to show up

Have expectations of deliverance. Look for God in every moment of your life.

How much time are you spending in prayer?

How many times have you taken this sin or weight before God's throne?

Have you told the Lord…"Yes Lord!"

A.R.R.E.S.T

Confess and praise every time you see God giving you strength and power against the enemy.

Insert your case:

T – Totally free! Free indeed! And Praise!
  *Everything about that defilement-Be offended
  *Hate the sin,
  *Hate the smell,
  *Hate the objects that represent or remind you,
  *Hate what it is doing to your life:mind (intellect), soul (spirit), and body (physical)

Fill your mind with the powerful scriptures of your deliverance.

A.R.R.E.S.T

Repeat the ARREST formula until you have no evidence of the sin, issue or attitude in your life. NOW BE FREE!

Let's touch and agree for your deliverance…

Matt 18:19-20 19 Again I say unto you, That if two of you shall agree on earth as touching any thing that they shall ask, it shall be done for them of my Father which is in heaven. 20 For where two or three are gathered together in my name, there am I in the midst of them. KJV

I'm going to pray with you now…

Lord, Jesus…Your name is so mighty and so powerful that there is nothing you can not do. We come to you Father, seeking for the power to be free.

Lord my sister (my brother) is tired of life the way it is. We agree and refuse to let things go on any longer. I pray for deliverance in your name just like you have told us to.

A.R.R.E.S.T

I pray the power of your word and promises would come down and forgive our sins and help us to forgive ourselves. For there is no condemnation in Christ Jesus. You can wash us until we no longer have memory of the pain that sin has caused us. We want to make up time for the time we lost being in sin.

We repent and ask you to cleanse us! Cleanse our minds from every influence of Satan and teach us how to fill our minds with things that will edify and not enslave our spirit man.

Lord we renounce Satan's ownership over our lives. Because when we live in sin he is our boss. We ask you to dismiss his power over us and humiliate him by doing a powerful deliverance in us. In Jesus' name. Father, teach us of your word so that we will be fully equipped to fight a good fight of faith and not allow Satan to trap us or hinder us again. Teach us thy way oh Lord and lead us in a plain path.

Thank you, Jesus. We glorify your holy name because your promises are true and never failing, we praise you for deliverance. We want to be free! We want our minds free, our hearts free, our spirit free, our homes free, our family free...in Jesus' name we pray and praise, AMEN!

NOW GO FORTH AND BE CHANGED IN THE NAME OF JESUS CHRIST!

John 8:36

If the Son therefore shall make you free, ye shall be free indeed. KJV

TESTIMONIALS

Rev 12:11

**11 And they overcame him by the blood of the Lamb , and by the word of their testimony; and they loved not their lives unto the death.
KJV**

TESTIMONIALS

After teaching the ARREST bible series several people approached me and shared how this revelation impacted them. Names were not revealed to protect privacy.

Formula D testimony: email

God bless you my Sister,

Thank you for saying plainly what one of my problems was and thank God He allowed me to truly hear. I tried at first to say that I needed a better understanding of what you were saying, but immediately, the Holy Ghost, brought back to me, you saying" after you or pastor says what God says, it's up to us to get to God and get the answer," so, I talked with God and He began to give me clarity on it. I went and slept with it on my mind. When I woke up this morning, I put on the first tape of the ARREST workshop and WOW! After, I prayed and the Lord showed me when I picked up this behavior, and why. I started when I was young, I felt I could do nothing right, and to please

A.R.R.E.S.T

my mom and everyone else that I feared or needed their approval, I would do whatever I felt necessary to please them whether or not I really wanted to just to be liked and accepted. The word came to me, "Whatsoever we do in word or deed, do all in the name Lord Jesus, giving thanks to God and the Father by him. Col. 3:17 And the other, Do as unto the Lord. I have been in bondage of doing things for approval of others and God has not been able to get the glory. I have to think about what pleases God. and be okay if I say no to something or someone it they don't feel alright with it, I am okay, God loves me, it's okay to be me! I feel like a new person. I even told my mom, that I will have to say no! God comes first.

I repented to God for everything and the Spirit of God came in and touched and O the Joy that floods my soul. I feel free and I am free!

Thank you for your ministry and patience. I can't say everything here, but thank you so much.

Your friend and spiritual daughter
Ir

A.R.R.E.S.T

Testimony:

I never seen hope the way the Lord revealed it in your teaching. It was amazing. I really needed that lesson.
dw

Testify of His goodness!

Formula D testimony: Personal testimony

One day after bible study a sister approached me with much excitement. She said that she wanted to tell me how ARREST had changed her life.

With great emotion she talked about how she could never believe that she could be delivered. She struggled with the things she did while in her sin and she couldn't receive the ministry call that she was hearing from God. She said that after learning about ARREST, especially after getting an understanding about the "RENOUNCE" step.

I went away praising God for blessing others through this revelation. This young lady was changed and her struggle with the past was over. Totally Delivered!

A.R.R.E.S.T

Testimony:

I sent your workshop version to some friends of mind and they said they were so blessed. I can't wait to send them your book.

A friend

Testimony:

One long time friend in New York came to me with his arms stretched in front of him with his wrists crossed as if handcuffed together. He looked to me and said, "CoPastor I still have it under arrest." I smiled and said, thank the Lord.

A fellow seeker

My Testimony:

The ARREST, formula for deliverance was a revelation given to me as I sought God for an answer to consistent holy living for those who may too frequently need to come to the altar and start again. The formula blessed me to become more constantly in a state of ministry readiness.

A.R.R.E.S.T

It is not a new revelation and I won't be promising it will solve all your problems. I will say that it works. It's just a strategy of deliverance, placed in a sequence that makes it easier to follow and remember. The ARREST, formula for deliverance in wonderful. I pray that all who read this book be blessed beyond measure.

clb

Glory and Praise to God!

A-R-R-E-S-T with Psalms 51

Ps 51:1-17

Have mercy upon me, O God, according to thy lovingkindness: according unto the multitude of thy tender mercies blot out my transgressions. 2 Wash me thoroughly from mine iniquity, and cleanse me from my sin. 3 For I acknowledge my transgressions: and my sin is ever before me. 4 Against thee, thee only, have I sinned, and done this evil in thy sight: that thou mightest be justified when thou speakest, and be clear when thou judgest. 5 Behold, I was shapen in iniquity; and in sin did my mother conceive me. 6 Behold, thou desirest truth in the inward parts: and in the hidden part thou shalt make me to know wisdom. 7 Purge me with hyssop, and I shall be clean: wash me, and I shall be whiter than snow. 8 Make me to hear joy and gladness; that the bones which thou hast broken may rejoice. 9 Hide thy face from my sins, and blot out all mine iniquities. 10 Create in me a clean heart, O God; and renew a right spirit within me. 11 Cast me not away from thy presence; and take not thy holy spirit from me. 12 Restore unto me the joy of thy salvation; and uphold me with thy free spirit. 13 Then will I teach transgressors thy ways; and sinners shall be converted unto thee.

14 Deliver me from bloodguiltiness, O God, thou God of my salvation: and my tongue shall sing aloud of thy righteousness. 15 O Lord, open thou my lips; and my mouth shall shew forth thy praise. 16 For thou desirest not sacrifice; else would I give it: thou delightest not in burnt offering. 17 The sacrifices of God are a broken spirit: a broken and a contrite heart, O God, thou wilt not despise. KJV

Psalm 51 has the formula for salvation, sanctification and deliverance. Read it again slowly and hear God give you the answers to your basics to live holy before God.

If this book has blessed you, write a testimony and send it me at
Joy of Life Ministries, Inc., 6401 N. 56th Street, Omaha, NE 68104

ABOUT THE AUTHOR

Evangelist/Co-Pastor Cynthia Lynette Butler

Evangelist Cynthia Butler is Co-Pastor and Vice President of Joy of Life Ministries, Inc. Cynthia is the second child of six to Florence and Donald Fancher. She has been the wife of Pastor Eric Butler for over 24 years. They have been blessed with three amazing children, Erica, Yvette and Jonathan.

Sister Butler gave her life to Christ at a young age and has been serving in ministry for over thirty-five years. After receiving the baptism in the Holy Ghost at the age of twelve she received her call to ministry as an evangelist. She has been a licensed evangelist through the Church of God in Christ since the age of 19 years old.

Evangelist Butler was given many opportunities to grow in ministry through the leadership of powerful men and women of God who have unselfishly mentored her. She will always be grateful.

Co-Pastor Cynthia partners with her husband in ministry at Joy of Life Ministries. She is Vice President of the corporate structure, Administrator of the ministry, Minister of Education and curriculum, and president of the Women of Excellence ministry. She fervently supports the vision of her husband, Pastor Eric.

Professionally, Cynthia Butler is an educator. She has a Bachelor's and Master's Degree in Elementary Education and a Master's Degree in Education Administration. In past years she has developed and facilitated after school programs in literacy and language arts to support students who struggle. She continues her mission as CEO and Director of the Purpose Driven Advocacy Center, Inc. which provides education and life advancing advocacy services to youth, adults and families. Her efforts have been acknowledged through many plaques, awards and nominations for special recognition. The Purpose Driven Advocacy Center, Inc. is a community service agency.

Co-Pastor Cynthia's ministry theme ~"Serving God by Serving His People."

Also ask about the "Triple CD set " of CoPastor Cynthia teaching the arrest revelation to the Joy of Life Bible Study.

Hear this concept in the fullness of biblical study. Each CD represents a service where ARREST was taught to increase faith in the promises of God and faith in the power of God.

Call or Write for your copy today to:

CoPastor Cynthia Butler, M.S. Edu. Admin.

Joy of Life Ministries

6401 N. 56th Street

Omaha, NE 68104

Or

Evangclb@aol.com

Or

402-399-9628

2/22/13 4:45A
Received Anointing to speak/pray in the Spirit.

Pray against
spirit of
confusion
slumber
slothfulness
procrastination
Cancelled
satan's Assignment
against me ∉
my family